H. C. Morrison, President Asbury College
(Front View of Administration Building.)

Commencement Sermons

Delivered in Asbury College Chapel

1913, 1914, 1915

by

Henry Clay Morrison

President of Asbury College

First Fruits Press
Wilmore, Kentucky
c2013

ISBN: 9781621711131

Commencement Sermons Delivered in Asbury College Chapel, 1913, 1914, 1915 / by H.C. Morrison.

First Fruits Press, © 2013
Louisville, Ky. : Pentecostal Publishing Company, c1915.
Digital version at
http://place.asburyseminary.edu/firstfruitsheritagematerial/25/

Morrison, H. C. (Henry Clay), 1857-1942.
    Commencement sermons delivered in Asbury college chapel, 1913, 1914, 1915 / by H.C. Morrison.
    Wilmore, Ky. : First Fruits Press, c2013.
    72 p. ; ill., port. ; 21 cm.
    The value of a soul -- Character building -- The Christ of the Gospel.
    Reprint. Previously published: Louisville, Ky. : Pentecostal Pub. Co., c1915.
    ISBN: 9781621711131 (pbk.)
    1. Baccalaureate addresses. I. Title. II. Asbury College (Wilmore, Ky.)
LD258 .A647 2013

Cover design by Haley Hill

asburyseminary.edu
800.2ASBURY
204 North Lexington Avenue
Wilmore, Kentucky 40390

First Fruits
THE ACADEMIC OPEN PRESS OF ASBURY SEMINARY

Commencement Sermons

Delivered in
Asbury College Chapel.

1913   1914   1915.

By

H. C. Morrison, D. D.,
President of Asbury College.

Copyrighted 1915 by

Pentecostal Publishing Company,
Louisville, Ky.

DEDICATION.

This collection of Commencement Sermons is affectionately Dedicated to the Board of Directors, Faculty, and Student body of Asbury College.

By the Author.

COMMENCEMENT SERMONS.

(1)

PREFACE.

It is my earnest hope that these Sermons, under the blessing of the Holy Spirit, may prove helpful to any, and everyone, who may read them.

They are bound up and sent forth in this form with a special prayer that they may prove helpful to the students of Asbury College, whom I love as a father loves his children.

Faithfully,

H. C. Morrison.

THE VALUE OF A SOUL.

(1913.)

Text: *"For what is a man profited, if he shall gain the whole world, and lose his own soul?"* Matt. 16:26.

Our Lord Jesus, in this text, introduces us into a realm of values where it is difficult, in fact impossible, for our mathematics to convey accurate conceptions.

If He had compared the value of a human soul to a splendid palace, we might go to the architects and builders who draw plans and erect structures, and get a very correct idea of the amount of money a palace would cost, setting down the figures, and adding up the columns, to ten, fifteen, or twenty millions of dollars; we could say, according to the statement of Jesus Christ, a human soul is worth more than all this.

If Jesus Christ had said, what shall a man be profited if he built, owned and controlled a great city, and lost his own soul, we might figure out, by consulting the proper authorities, something approximating the cost of a great city, with all its manufacturing interests, business center, residential district, its street car system, light plant, waterworks, skyscrapers, and the vast aggregation of material wealth that goes into the making of a great city, climbing into the tens and hundreds of millions, and billions of wealth; then we could add up the figures and say, according to Jesus Christ, a man would make a bad bargain if he possessed himself of a great city and lost his own soul.

If Jesus had said, what shall it profit a man if he gain an entire continent and lose his soul, we would then have a diffi-

The Value of a Soul.

cult task on our hands if we undertook
to figure out, with any sort of accuracy,
the value of a continent, with its great
farming regions, its mineral resources,
its vast forests, its railroad systems and
steamship lines, its many investments
and industries, its villages, towns and
cities. To fix any sort of correct esti-
mate upon such incalculable wealth
would be almost impossible.

Come to think of it, a humble farmer
cannot tell the actual value of his land.
Not long since I was riding with an expert who was employed to locate coal
lands. He said to me that up in Vir-
ginia there was an old farmer who owned some two hundred acres of land so
poor that he could scarcely earn a mea-
ger sustenance from its lean and rocky
soil. He said on investigation he had
found that some hundreds of feet beneath the soil there was a vein of ex-
cellent coal, four feet thick, that was
worth a vast sum of money, and that a

few hundred feet below this vein of coal there was a vein of candle coal, eleven feet thick, which was so rich that it could be lighted with a match.

The farmer little dreamed that his possessions were worth hundreds of thousands of dollars; that some day the company the expert represented proposed to buy the poor tract of land and gather from beneath its surface the vast treasures of which its owner knew nothing. I remarked to the enthusiastic young expert, that beneath the candle coal there might be great reservoirs of oil, and beneath the oil marvelous values in gas, and beneath the gas there might be deposits of silver, and beneath the silver, veins of gold, and down deep toward the eternal fires there might be priceless diamonds. He seemed to become amazed and embarrassed as I mentioned the possibilities of wealth beneath the surface of the poor old farm, over which he chuckled at the thought of buying. No, it is impossible for us to figure out the value of a continent. It would run into the millions, billions, and hundreds of billions, and yet, we have not reached the value of a soul.

The Lord Jesus Christ was the only being who ever came out of the infinitudes and walked the paths of human life, who really knew the value of a soul. He is the only one who ever walked among us, and talked to us, who has seen a soul, who understands its marvelous capacities, its wondrous beauty and powers. When He came to our earth He saw at once that men had no proper appreciation of soul values. He saw that we thought souls were a very good thing to crowd into the dust and grime of factories and sweatshops, to wear out with incessant toil, to huddle into the deep mines of the earth, and smother with poisonous gases; to march into saloons and degrade with strong drink, that swaggering distillers and brewers

(9)

may become millionaires, to catch in the traps of white slavery and send away into wretchedness, ruin, and perdition. He saw that man, in his miscalculation, thought that souls were a fine thing to gather from their homes, shops, villages, colleges and universities, throw them into squads, drill them into companies, form them into regiments, weld them into great armies, ship them away from native lands and drive them against rapid-fire guns, hurl them against walls of bayonets, and pour them like a human Niagara into the black pits of outer darkness.

Jesus desired to arrest our attention and awaken in us some sort of proper appreciation of the value of a human soul. He looked about Him for a comparison to convey to our minds some conception of its worth. Palaces were as nothing; cities and continents were not large enough; the world itself was too small to convey a correct idea of the

The Value of a Soul.

fearful blunder a man would make if he should gain this entire planet, with all the wealth on and in it, and lose his own soul.

Think of it! According to the statements of the only One who has ever been in our midst, who has a proper appreciation of values, if you had a scale large enough to put into one end a human soul, and in the other end your prosperous, beautiful little city, and then you put in Louisville, Cincinnati, Cleveland, St. Louis, Kansas City, Denver, San Francisco, Los Angeles, Houston, New Orleans, Nashville, Charleston, S. C., Richmond, Va., Washington City, Baltimore, Philadelphia, New York, Boston, Glasgow, Scotland, London, Paris, Berlin, St. Petersburg, Bombay, Calcutta, Yokahoma, Peking, China, and old Jerusalem—one soul would outweigh them all. Not the soul of Moses, St. Paul, Martin Luther, John Wesley, Wm. Shakespeare, Queen Victoria, Frances Willard, or any other great intellect that ever blessed the world, but the soul of a sick and starving baby in the bony arms of a heathen mother, in the jungles of India.

These words of Jesus awaken in us a thoughtful inquiry into the most interesting subject that can claim our attention. What is a soul? We should not be surprised if, after all, man is God's greatest creation. At the present time no doubt the angels have advantages over us ,but they are older than we. As the centuries roll along we may overtake and pass them in the scale of being. We notice that we were created after their creation; and we have not noticed that in His work the Lord tapers down from the larger to the smaller things. After He had created the heavens, and rolled the planets from His finger-tips, and prepared the earth for habitation, He said, "Let us make man in our own image." We have not read in the inspired Book that He spoke thus of any other being He brought into existence. We hear the Psalmist David saying, "When I consider thy heavens, the work of thy fingers, the moon and the stars, which thou hast ordained; What is man, that thou art mindful of him? and the son of man, that thou visitest him? For thou hast made him a little lower than the angels, and hast crowned him with glory and honor. Thou madest him to have dominion over the works of thy hands: thou hast put all things under his feet."

We are told that the literal translation of the Hebrew is: "Thou hast made him less than God." We are also taught that angels are our guardians; and Paul tells us that we shall judge angels. Mark you, we are not seeking to depreciate angels, but these words of the Lord Jesus with regard to the value of a soul put one to thinking and wondering where man's place is among the intelligences of God's creation.

(13)

Commencement Sermons.

It will be well to remember that the human soul is immortal. We value things on the basis of their durability. After the furnaces of the suns have burned into cinders, and the stars have fallen like the withering leaves of a fig tree, your soul will be rising upon the wings of immortal youth into the glorious heights of a topless heaven and an endless eternity.

The Lord has permitted us to catch some glimpses of the marvelous capacity of the human soul. Some years ago there lived in our community a young negro, an uneducated boy, whose mathematical bump seemed not to have been damaged by the fall. He was a lightning calculator. You could propound to him the most difficult mathematical problems, and almost instantly he would answer you with marvelous accuracy. He did not understand how he did it, but he did it without difficulty. It is possible that, but for sin, we never would have had to learn the multiplication table, or waste time with lead pencil and chalk, knitting our brows over difficult mathematical problems. We are not willing to believe that he was any sort of monstrosity, but by some mysterious means he had the remnant of intellectual power that might have belonged to us all, but for sin.

Many years ago Jenny Lind came to this country. At her first entertainment in Grand Opera in New York, the people paid large sums of money for the privilege of hearing her. She sang until you would forget that you were sick. She sang until you would forget your debts. She sang until you would forget your enemies. She sang until you forgave everybody and loved everybody. She sang until it seemed as if you were lifted into heaven. She sang until she was transfigured before you and seemed to be an angel. We believe if it had not been for sin, had our vocal chords not been jarred out of tune by wicked speech, harsh words and profanity, we would have such singers everywhere. These marvelous gifts and greater await us on yonder golden shore, when we are released from our captivity and come into our own.

Traveling the rugged paths of life, and fighting out the problems on the battle-field here, I have often longed to sing, but have never been able to bring my jargon voice into harmony with sweet melody; but I know that I *shall sing.* I feel the heavenly anthems within my breast that in yonder world shall break forth into immortal songs of praise.

The Scriptures plainly teach that when we have passed through the tragedy of death and the glorious mysteries of the resurrection, we shall rise on the other side in the likeness of our Lord. You remember that Moses went up into the mountain and stayed with God for

(16)

forty days and nights, and when he came down his countenance shone with such brightness that he must needs be covered with a veil that the people might endure such glory. Suppose he had remained with his God for a year! What must his appearance have been when he descended among the people! Looking into the future state with the prophet's ken, David picked up his harp and sang, "I shall be satisfied when I awake in thy likeness." And John, the Beloved, has written in his Epistle, "Beloved, now are we the sons of God, and it doth not yet appear what we shall be: but we know that when He shall appear, we shall be like Him; for we shall see Him as He is."

With these Scriptures before us we can begin to appreciate that the spiritual is of infinitely more value than the material; that the immortal is incomparably greater than the transcient; that mere dirt, cinders, gold, and diamonds of earth will not compare with that intelligence which lays hold upon the infinite and walks in fellowship and sweet communion with the God of the universe.

The human soul is capable of holiness. It is unthinkable that an infinitely wise and good God would create an immortal, responsible being incapable of a state of moral purity. It must be remembered that sin is not an essential part of human nature. God created man in a state of holiness; sin was introduced into his nature later on. Sin was the work of the devil. Jesus Christ was manifested to destroy the works of the devil. All sin can be eliminated from the soul without the destruction or hurt of any of its essential qualities. The removal of sin leaves the human soul in its normal and original state of purity and oneness with God.

This is the whole purpose and end of the redemptive scheme—to separate

The Value of a Soul.

from man that which separated him
from communion and oneness with his
Maker. This is redemption. All pro-
phecy, all priests and sacrifices, all the
manifestations and sufferings of the
Lord Jesus, all the writings of the Apos-
tles, the great purpose and end of the
church is to bring a race, fallen and
sinful, back into perfect harmony with
the infinite will, and into perfect love of
the infinite Being.

If an old man from the backwoods,
who never saw the ocean, who never
looked upon a ship, a boat, a skiff, a
canoe, or any sort of watercraft, should
come out of the woods upon the ocean
beach and look with amazement upon
th evast expanse of waves; if he should
see lying in the sand half buried, a
wrecked ship, and if he should ask some
old sailor standing by, "What is this object before me?" and the sailor should
say, "that is a ship;" the old man from
the backwoods would exclaim, "that a

ship! Is that what you traverse the sea in? Can you carry commerce and passengers across the vast ocean in that sort of thing?" The old sailor would answer him, "that is a wrecked ship. That is the ruin of a great vessel that went down in triumph, to the sea." The old sailor would tell him of the splendid structure, of its length, and breadth, and depth; of its staunch timbers and iron sides, its graceful masts and powerful engines, and how it plowed the main as a thing of life. Then he would tell him how the storm tossed it, and the waves beat upon it, and the rocks rent it, and the lightning splintered it, and the billows flung it, wrecked, upon the shore. Looking upon that wreck the old man from the woods would have a poor conception of the splendid strength and beauty the great ocean steamer presented before the tempest rent and wrecked it.

Just so it is with man. We have never seen a man. We have seen what is left of him. We have seen him after the waves of sin have dashed him, bruised and broken him along the rocky shores of time. We have seen him after the dirt and sand and grit of sin have been ground into him, defaced and marred him.

The Lord Jesus Christ saw him when he came complete in purity and beauty from the creative hand of God. He saw him before he gave a listening ear to the seductive voice of the tempter, before sin had stamped its foul insignia upon his spotless spirit. In that far-off day he was a godlike being. The Son of God loved him with a great deep, eternal affection, and when he went astray in the paths of sin and ruin, He followed him. Followed him when it meant poverty, suffering, humiliation, a crown of thorns, derision and hatred, the cross with its agony and shame. He followed him like the good shepherd, seeking a lost and wolf-torn sheep, to bind up his wounds and lay him upon the omnipotent shoulders of His mightiness to save to the uttermost.

No price, from the standpoint of the Lord Jesus, was too large to pay; no suffering was too severe to bear; no death agony was too bitter to meet and undergo. Thank God, He solved the problem. He knew the value of human souls and He drank the cup of sorrow and suffering to its last bitter dregs. Standing in the midst of sinful men, He looked back to their original state of purity and godlikeness. He gazed into the eternities of unfolding grace and glory, and as He contemplated man's origin and the possibilities of his redemption and the eternal future—as He weighed these possibilities and destinies he exclaimed, "What shall it profit a man if he shall gain the whole world, and lose his own soul?"

At the close of His mission and ministry here, hanging pale and bleeding on a Roman cross, He bowed His head and said, "It is finished." A bridge of redemption and human hope stretched like a mighty arch across the centuries from the fall of Adam in the Garden of Eden to the death of Jesus Christ on the hill of Calvary; over that bridge multitudes and millions have been coming back to God and home to heaven. And when the end shall have come at last, and the immaculate and ever adorable Redeemer shall stand in the midst of those redeemed by the sacrificial blood which He shed upon Calvary's rugged brow, "He shall see of the travail of His soul, and shall be satisfied."

In yonder world when we behold the unfolding, development and progress of human souls—the "exceeding and eternal weight of glory"—we shall be prepared to appreciate more fully the deep meaning of the text, "For what is a man profited if he shall gain the whole world, and lose his own soul?"

CHARACTER BUILDING.

(1914)

"Benaiah the son of Jehoiada, the son of a valiant man of Kabzeel, who had done many acts; he slew two lionlike men of Moab; also he went down and slew a lion in a pit in a snowy day. And he slew an Egyptian, a man of great stature, five cubits high; and in the Egyptian's hand was a spear like a weaver's beam; and he went down to him with a staff, and plucked the spear out of the Egyptian's hand and slew him with his own spear." (1 Chron. 11:22, 23).

In our devotional reading, not long since, we fell upon these verses which struck us with peculiar force and awakened in our mind quite a train of thought. As we mused, looking back through the centuries, we seemed to see this man, Benaiah, who proved himself more than equal to any of the enemies that came up against him, standing befor us. Unpleasant as it may be, even with the eye of the imagination, to look upon deadly strike between men, it was interesting to see him slay those two lionlike fellows of Moab. When the Bible says "lionlike men" you may be sure they were stalwart, determined, fearless fighters.

The record also tells us of this man Benaiah, that "he went down and slew a lion in a pit in a snowy day." We take it that the lion could have been left in the pit until the snow melted away, and there would have been less danger of slipping or losing one's footing in a contest with so dangerous a foe; or he might have been left there to starve; or he might have been pelted to death with stones from the top of the pit. But this man Benaiah looked into the pit with sparkling eyes and tightening muscles, and slid down its snowy side to meet the king of beasts face to face, and the record says, "he slew him."

The inspired writer does not tell us what Benaiah had in his hands on the occasion of taking such dangerous risk; possibly a spear or club. We have an idea he clubbed the royal beast to death. It is interesting to stand in imagination at the top of the pit and watch this brawny warrior as he fearlessly approaches his roaring enemy and, with agility, avoids the lion's leap and strikes him a deathblow as he passes.

On another occasion he meets up with an Egyptian of great stature, "five cubits high." He is carrying a spear with a staff like a weaver's beam; a load for an ordinary man. He went down to meet this giant with no weapon in his hand save a staff—a mere walking cane.

Striding forward with easy, resolute step he meets him in a hand-to-hand conflict, wrenches the spear away from him, pitches him off, and pinions him with his own weapon.

David had a very remarkable aggregation of men in his army at this time. You remember that during one of his wars, while the enemy held Bethlehem, David expressed a desire for a drink of water from a well in that village, and three of his sturdy warriors fought their way through the ranks of the enemy, who held the village at the time, drew water from the well and, fighting their way back into David's camp, presented him with the water. You recall that David refused to drink it, but poured it upon the ground in sacrifice.

Since our childhood, we have taken pleasure in closing our eyes and looking at those three, fearless soldiers. What iron-like faces they must have had; what strong limbs, what muscular arms and blazing eyes; what tremendous blows they struck; what a flying wedge they made flinging the ranks of the enemy apart. How fearlessly two of them stood as statues at bay with drawn swords, while the third dropped his bucket into the well and brought up the cool, dripping water; with what insolence they strode away, with lips curled in smiles of contempt; the drops of water falling from their bucket writing in wet hieroglyphics in the dust their derision of their foes. These were no ordinary men. They were men for their times. War was not the scientific game that it is today; it was not a question of telescope, range finder, raised sights, an accurate eye, and the motion of a finger. It was not the dropping of an explosive shell from some craft in the upper air. The successful soldier of David's day must be a man of great physical power. He must be able to strike sledge-hammer blows, quick and fast. Strength, agility, and animal courage went into the making of the winning men of the times. Of course, there were bows and arrows and stones for the sling, but much of the war of those days was a grim meat-ax proposition.

These three men cutting their way into and out of Bethlehem, for that drink of water for David would make a moving picture worth looking upon. Our friend of the text has a peculiar fascination for us; not that we have any delight in bloodshed, or even the death of dumb creatures, but when giant Moabites must be dealt with, and there is a roaring lion plunging about in his fury in a pit in a snowy day, who needs attention, we delight in a fearless fellow who is ready for the emergency and is easily the master of the situation

David lived in a day when God had some cleaning up to do. He was clearing the ground of unbelief and wickedness. He was sweeping away a people who would make no progress, and who stood in the way of those who desired to go forward. They were unfit to propagate the race, to put their mental and moral stamp upon posterity. God desired the space they occupied for the raising up and development of a better race of people, and David and his big, fearless, brawny soldiers were the men to meet the requirements of the hour.

There has not been a time in human history so dull, dead, and insignificant that some tragedy in the life and progress of the race has not occupied the stage of action. And whatever the emergency of the hour, God has had His men who could meet the evils and difficulties to be contended with, as Benaiah met the giants of Moab, who would dare to go down into the pits of human struggle and sacrifice, taking their lives in their hands and coming out conquerors. (31)

Our friend of the text, it occurs to us, was possessed of a certain kind of self-confidence in a remarkable degree. Not egotism, not pride, or self-conceit, but something entirely different; a quality that must exist in every man who achieves success. We dare say he had a restful faith in God, and a consciousness that he was in the divine service and endued with a divine power. He went to meet the giants of Moab; he climbed down into the pit to face the lion and sauntered out, walking cane in hand, to meet and vanquish the big Egyptian without a tremor of fear, but a strong faith in God and a full assurance of and enduement of strength within his own great arm to accomplish the task which had fallen to him to perform.

There is something delightful in the contemplation of a true, godly, fearless man, who feels in his soul that he has a work to perform in the world, and with-

out boast or bluster, without hesitation
or fear, goes forward, meets the difficulties, overcomes the obstacles, con-
quers his foes and does his work.

We get comfort and courage in contemplation of this strong man of long
ago, and we get valuable suggestions.
There are always giants to kill, and
lions to club, and evils swaggering
about with spears whose staffs are large
as weavers' beams. There are gigantic
errors in the world to be slain, and
they must be slain or the world will become impossible of habitation. It occurs to us that there has been no time
within a century, when there was
greater need of real men trusting in
God, conscious of union with Him, and
conscious of power within themselves
because of this union, to meet and battle
successfully with the serious problems
with which we are confronted in our
day and generation. There is, per-
haps, no greater work in which we

can engage than the building, equipping and sending forth of men, soldiers of the cross, the foundation stone of whose character is laid in an unshakable faith in God and in the Bible. Men with Christian experience, experience that gives them undoubted and abiding rest of soul, who have enlisted in the army of righteousness to fight on and on until the war is over. Spiritual soldiers of fortune, who are on the alert and looking for opportunities to employ their God given powers in slaying the giants of evil and beating to pulp the heads of the savage beasts of sin.

Reading of this man Benaiah has set us reflecting on those qualities that should go into the making up of sturdy, aggressive, fearless Christian manhood, manhood that will be able to go up against the Moabites of unbelief and the giants of wickedness. Those qualities that will put moral nerve and muscle into the champions of truth and righteousness, which will equip men, without hesitation, to go down into the pits of human ruin and combat the lions of greed and vice and all the rampant forms of modern wickedness, and slay them.

How can we produce the men and the women to do this work? What qualities and equipment are necessary that we may send forth sturdy, victorious conquerors for God—men and women who can salt the earth, illuminate the world, uplift society, preserve faith in the Bible, reverence for the Sabbath, the purity of the home, the sanctity of the church and build the dykes and bulwarks that will hold in check the mad waves of the ocean of worldliness that beat with fury upon the boundary line of all that is sacred and holy, and would engulf and sweep away all that magnifies the Christ and brings peace and happiness to the human race.

First of all, such men must be Christians. They must know God and commune with Him. They must be in touch with Jesus Christ; they must be filled with the Spirit. Give a man an assurance that he came from the Creator of all things, that he had his origin in the thought and purpose of the Almighty, that he has a mission in the world, that the divine hand holds him, that the divine wisdom illuminates him, that infinite resources are at his command and call, that the divine approval will crown him at the end of the conflict, and you will doubtless have a man of unshaken faith, fearless soul, enlarged vision, fixed purpose; a man of action, a moral and spiritual hero, who will face and fight your giants of evil and your beasts of sin without a tremor. You will have a man who will undertake that, which to the ordinary and commonplace, seems impossible and, by the grace of God, he will triumph.

Second, they must be educated men.

Character Building.

Their thinking powers must be developed, their mental faculties must be trained. They must know how to concentrate and direct their energies to the best purpose.

We grant you readily, that the human race is a fallen race; that the human heart is corrupt; that man is a frail, changeful, and sinful being, but you must grant us that man was created in the image of God; that when he fell divine love followed him; that to redeem, reinstate and bring him back into harmony and co-operation with his maker, Jesus Christ came out of Heaven, tramped the rugged path of life and in tears, agony and blood, found the lost sheep which had gone astray. He made possible the new birth. He opened the way to the highest privilege of the crucifixion of the carnal nature. He came to stamp upon man again the divine image, to separate and cleanse him from sin and restore him to God.

Commencement Sermons.

This is a great salvation which Jesus
Christ has wrought out for the race.
Hanging upon the Cross on Calvary, He
not only saw the mob that gathered
about His feet in the wild excitement of
blind vengeance, but He looked afar and
saw the spread of the gospel, the uplift
of the fallen, the redemption of the lost.
He saw the prodigals coming home to
the father's house. He saw the ignorant become illuminated with knowledge,
the sinful become holy, the weak and
faltering become strong and courageous.
He saw the kingdoms of this world become the kingdoms of our Lord and His
Christ. He saw the glad and glorious
day when the knowledge of the glory
of the Lord shall cover the earth as the
waters cover the sea.

He not only heard the shout of the
mob and the jeer of the wild and wicked
multitude, but He heard the prayers
of the millions. He heard the songs of
joy and shouts of victory. He heard a

redeemed world lifting its voice in one grand anthem of praise until the foundations of the kingdom of Satan and sin were shaken and fallen into hopeless ruin. He heard the choirs of His redeemed Church circling the globe with the glad song,

"Jesus, the name high over all,
  In earth, or hell or sky;
Angels and men before it fall,
  And devils fear and fly."

If we want spiritual Benaiahs in the world, broad-shouldered, sure-footed, strong-armed men, who can be relied upon to stand up against, drive back and beat down the evils that would destroy our country and our people, we must make men acquainted with the Christ; they must come into communion with Him; they must love Him supremely; they must make His cross their cross, His life their life, His mission their mission, the great purpose and end of His suffering and triumph their suffering and their triumph.

To build such men is the greatest work that can employ the energies, busy the thoughts and claim the beneficence of human beings. This is the work of Asbury College. It was with this end in view that this school had its beginning. There were other schools which taught grammar, mathematics, science, history, philosophy and religion. They have broad stretches of campus, stately and classic structures, liberal endowments and history of usefulness and renown; but there was needed another school in the land with broader vision and higher purpose than any other school existing in all the country. An institution was needed that laid special stress upon Bible study; that called its student body to true repentance for sin; that urged upon its young manhood and womanhood the necessity of the new birth; that set before its entire student body the highest standard of Christian holiness; that exalted the Lord Jesus Christ as one mighty to save to the uttermost; that believed that the Bible, Old Testament and New, is an inspired revelation from God, and that the Christianity it proclaims is practical and is the only hope for the human race.

Within a few hundred yards of the spot where we now stand, a group of patient and sturdy souls, almost a quarter of a century ago, erected a small, wooden structure of four rooms, threw it together rapidly amidst cheerful songs and earnest prayer, and filled those four rooms with brawny, sunburned lads, who had wrestled, Jacob like, with the Lord, and who had won the greatest victory possible to man. They had won the assurance of the forgiveness of sin, and they had won the inward consciousness of the crucifixion of the carnal nature, the incoming and

(41)

abiding of the Holy Ghost. They had
struggled out of the darkness of doubt
into the clear, abiding sunlight of a full
assurance of faith. They had been
filled with a pr~..und conviction that
they were called of God to preach the
gospel that had brought to them such
wonderful deliverance.

It was only two dozen years ago that
the hammers of this consecrated group
constructing the little four-room building rang out their challenge to the
blighting unbelief and worldliness of the
times. Two dozen years have fled away
and behold, what God hath wrought!
Thousands of earnest souls have gathered here from every quarter of the nation and from beyond the seas. This
little village has become a world-famed
center of spiritual light, intellectual development, evangelistic and missionary
influence. The plant has grown from
year to year until its proportions are
larger than the faith of those who love
it best.   (42)

Character Building.

Its student body, the most loyal and devoted beneath the stars, has gone abroad carrying the message of full salvation to the enus of the earth. The students of Asbury College have entered successfully the various walks of life—lawyers, physicians, dentists, merchants, mechanics. They may be found scattered throughout the country, prosperous, successful and happily bearing witness to the power of Jesus Christ to save from sin. Asbury College rejoices in the fact that she has sent out a host of teachers into universities, colleges and public schools, who breathe the spirit of prayer and faith, and everywhere dropped the seeds of gospel truth into the fertile soil of young and aspiring souls; but she rejoices with profoundest gratitude over her sons and daughters who have given themselves to the ministry of the Lord Jesus Christ; her sturdy pastors, her flaming evangelists, her faithful missionaries, scattered throughout the nation and around the world, carrying into India, China, Japan, Korea, Africa, South America, Porto Rico, and the Philippine Islands the glad good news, that in Jesus Christ there is bounteous redemption full and free for all men from all sin.

At these Commencement Exercises we look back over the two dozen years of our history with gratitude and thanksgiving to God, and we look forward with increased faith and larger vision and gird ourselves afresh to undertake more for Him who gave Himself for us, and to expect larger blessings from Him to whom we consecrate ourselves for a more devoted service. We appeal to the board of faithful and devoted men, who love and labor for the enlargement and progress of this institution. We appeal to the student body which has been blessed through her influence; we appeal to devout men and women everywhere, who love the Bible and the pure gospel, the cause of Christian holiness and of missions, to rally to our standards, to help us enlarge this plant, increase its usefulness, continue its energetic efforts to reach the ends of the earth with the great gospel for which it stands, and most of all, to remember us in prayer for the blessings of the adorable Trinity to abide upon this place and all the work in which we are engaged for the uplift and blessing of humanity.

THE CHRIST OF THE GOSPEL.

(1915.)

"Without controversy great is the mystery of godliness: God was manifest in the flesh, justified in the Spirit, seen of angels, preached unto the Gentiles, believed on in the world, received up into glory." 1st Tim. 3:16.

The inspired writers nowhere undertake to explain the mysteries which abound in the revelations God has made to man. It must be understood that the revelation of the divine Being—the incarnation of Jesus Christ—and the new and holy life of peace and joy which come to those who trust in Him cannot be figured out and explained by mathematical processes or in terms of human philosophy. We would call your attention to the fact, that it is not necessary to enter the realm of divine revelation and our Christian religion in order to find mysteries; we are surrounded with mysteries. There are many things with which we come in constant contact which we cannot understand. Who can explain to us electricity? We know it exists; it is about us everywhere; it illuminates our pathway with its light; its penetrating rays may destroy germs and heal us of disease. We may cook our food with its heat. It leaps across the ocean carrying our message with the speed of lightning, but Edison himself cannot tell us what electricity is.

Prof. Huxley once wrote: "The mysteries of the Church are child's play compared with the mysteries of nature. The doctrine of the trinity is no more puzzling than the necessary antinomies of physical speculation; virgin procreation and resuscitation from apparent

(48)

death are ordinary phenomenon for the naturalist." If men propose to reject what they cannot understand, they will have to reject not only the mysteries of the spiritual world, but the mysteries of the natural world as well, for all nature about us is full of problems that have not been solved.

"Great is the mystery of godliness." Angels at the present time are doubtless far more intelligent than men, and yet the angels cannot fully comprehend the profound and deep secrets which are shut up in the council of the infinite trinity. David was an inspired man, but David said: "Such knowledge is too wonderful for me; it is high, I cannot attain to it."

To the devout Christian who believes the Bible, loves Jesus Christ and worships God in spirit and in truth, the mysteries connected with our holy religion are not an objection, but a fascination, always claiming reverential study and constantly increasing our spiritual comprehension of divine goodness and the glorious plan of human redemption.

The Apostle Paul beautifully reconciles us to present conditions when he writes in 1st Cor. 13:12, "For now we see through a glass, darkly; but then face to face: now I know in part; but then shall I know even as also I am known."

Much of the destructive criticism of the times, which is producing widespread unbelief and contributing in a thousand ways to the increase of wickedness in the world, arises out of the fact that modern scholarship has produced among men an intellectual pride that scorns the simple faith of the devout child of God and purposes, by mere human philosophies, to solve all mysteries connected with the immaculate conception, the divine incarnation, the resurrection and the power of the sacrificial blood of the Holy Christ to lift sinful men out of a state of degradation and depravity into a state of sanctification and oneness with the eternal Father.

There is nothing more marvelous in all the realm of revelation than the incarnation of Jesus Christ. The inspired writer says truly: "Without controversy great is the mystery of godliness. God was manifest in the flesh."

The rebellion and fall of man into a state of sinfulness brought so wide a separation between him and the infinitely holy God, the condition was so hopeless, the distance separating the two beings apart was so wide, the chasm so vast and deep, that in order to bridge it there must be brought into existence a mediator between God and man. Divine wisdom conceived the plan, and divine wisdom never rose to higher heights, or stooped to deeper depths of compassionate love than in the solving of the sin problem, rescuing man from his fallen condition and restoring him to a state of holiness and communion with his Maker. In accomplishing this great work, infinite wisdom found it necessary to combine two natures in one being. Man's condition was such that it was necessary to offer him a Redeemer so human that He could sympathize with him, and so divine that He could save him.

God had created men, but He had never been a man. God had seen men toil, but He had never blistered His hand with carpenter's tools. He had seen men weep, but He had never wept. He had seen men struggling in the midst of temptation, but He had never felt the onslaughts of the tempter against Himself. He had seen men bleed, but He had never bled. He had seen the millions struggling on the crumbling verge of the grave, and finally sinking into its hopeless depths, but He had never felt the cold grip of death, or spread

The Christ of The Gospel.

His omnipotent shoulders upon the bottom of a sepulchre. He determined, because it was a necessity, in the discovery and opening up the way for a lost and sinful race to return to purity, peace, and fellowship with Himself, to come into the world, to take the weight of humanity upon Himself, to walk its rugged paths, to carry its heavy burdens, to know its deep sorrows and heart-breaking griefs, to meet and conquor its tempter and destroyer, to suffer and die among its outcasts and criminals, to lie down in the house of death, and then to arise in majesty and rend the gate of the tomb asunder, opening the way for a redeemed race from the grave to the glorious resurrection and eternal life.

The wisdom of the incarnation is seen when we remember how difficult it is for the finite to grasp the infinite, for the earthly to comprehend the heavenly, for the sinful to approach the holy.

It is hard for us to fix our thoughts upon that great Being without body or parts, who is eternal in existence, omnipotent in power, and omnipresent. The poor human intellect staggers with the thought. We do not know where to begin, how to proceed, or where to leave off. The wings of our imagination grow weary, the brain grows dizzy, while the heart hungers on, and we are made to cry out in the language of Job: "Canst thou by searching find out God? Canst thou find out the Almighty unto perfection? It is as high as heaven; what canst thou do? deeper than hell; what canst thou know? The measure thereof is longer than the earth, and broader than the sea."

It is easy to think of the Babe of Bethlehem, and with the wise men to worship Him. Even in His infancy lying in a manger, He was a true object of worship. There is no intimation that the gathering of the eastern sages and the humble shepherds on bended knees about that wondrous child was sacrilege. It is delightful to stand amidst priests and doctors of the law, listening to His wisdom, while He is yet a youth; to go down to John's baptism and see Him standing meek and lowly in the presence of the rugged preacher, and saying: "Suffer it to be so now, for thus it becometh us to fulfill all righteousness." It thrills us to follow Him up the mountain side, to look with awe upon the temptation. The Second Adam has met with the foe before whom the first Adam fell, and we behold with joy the defeat of Satan, and the triumph of the world's Redeemer. We can trail Him along His pathway by the crutches and the canes which have been cast aside by the halt and lame He has healed, and the shouts and praises of those from whom devils have been cast out.

As we follow Him there is no doubt

that He is God manifest in the flesh. He walks like a man, but He works like a God. We behold His humanity when He lay sleeping in the boat, and His deity when He arises and rebukes the wind and storm, and the tempest sinks into silence at His command. He weeps like a man at Lazarus' tomb, but with godlike voice He breaks the power of death and brings him forth alive. As a man, He sits hungry at the well's mouth; like a God, He breaks the few loaves and little fishes and feeds the multitude. Like a man, He goes into the mountains for prayer; like a God He walks the waves of the sea of Galilee and overtakes His disciples who have gone forth in the ship. Like a man, He climbs the mountain; transfigured like a God He stands upon its crest in garments whiter than the light.

What a marvelous combination of the two natures—human and divine! Spirit begotten and virgin born. The eternal

(56)

Spirit did not beget a *thing*, but a person. He did not beget an animal, but a man. There is no teaching further from the tenor of the Holy Scriptures than that the visible Christ was some sort of strange creature, without human nature, mind or soul. Jesus had a human mind, which "grew in knowledge." He had a human soul, of which He said in Gethsemane, "My soul is exceeding sorrowful, even unto death."

In coming to the World's Redeemer, seeking to know something of Him and what He means to the world, and what He is to us, the Holy Scriptures weigh infinitely more with us than all the reasonings and philosophies of men. They have absolute right-of-way. Turning to the Scriptures we find the inspired writer saying, "For verily He took not on Him the nature of angels; but He took on Him the seed of Abraham." That is, the nature of man. And again,

"Wherefore in all things it behooved Him to be made like unto His brethren, that He might be a merciful and faithful high priest in things pertaining to God, to make reconciliation for the sins of the people. For in that He Himself hath suffered, being tempted, He is able to succour them that are tempted."

J. G. Holland, in his sweetest poem, strikes the keynote of the gospel when he says: "Tempted in every point like as ourselves was He tempted, yet without sin. It was through temptation, thought I, that the Lord, the mediator between God and man, reached down the sympathetic hand of love to meet the grasp of lost humanity." It is through the knowledge of this human kinship that men are enabled to approach, trust in, and claim the mercy of Christ. It is through His humanity that we approach the Son, and it is through the Son that we come to the Father. Jesus says, "No man cometh to the Father but by me." "No man knoweth the Father, save the Son, and He to whom the Son will reveal Him."

It is by means of this divine Christ, who was made like unto His brethren in body, mind, and soul, that the wide chasm stretching between an infinitely holy God and an utterly depraved and fallen man is bridged; our Redeemer becomes to us a faithful "high priest who can be touched with the feelings of our infirmities," and yet possessing in Himself that eternal power and godhead which make Him one and equal with the Father, able to save to the uttermost.

It is an inspiration to contemplate that great painting of Michael Angelo on the ceiling of the Sistine Chapel at Rome. In the picture he makes the Master to stand before the beholder "As the head of all humanity, as the goal of all progress, as the consummation of all glory." This picture has been called the most eloquent of all sermons, on Christ communing with the whole world. Standing in the presence of that picture, one's heart is thrilled as he contemplates the mysterious union of the two natures into one being, and seems to be looking upon the majesty and beauty of combined humanity and deity.

The conflict of the centuries has raged around Jesus Christ. He was unknown until He was manifest in the flesh, and the Father was unknown—that is, He was never understood—until He was revealed in the Son. The world had heard of the eternal God. He had revealed Himself to a few men; the prophets had proclaimed His laws for our government, angels had now and again brought some message from the headquarters of the universe, but God was unknown until Jesus came, walked in our midst and communed with us. He sat down, ate with sinners, touched elbows with profane and wicked men, healed our sick, made our lame to leap for joy, our deaf to hear the tender melodies of His compassionate voice. He forgave those detected in the vilest sins, and everywhere and always lived on the highest plane of holiness and breathed the sweetest spirit of compassion and mercy.

When the disciples insisted that He should show them the Father, He said, "He that hath seen me hath seen the Father." What amazing words are these! We never could have had any such conception of the eternal God of the ages. We knew He could build a universe, fling the stars from His fingertips into their orbits, but we never dreamed that He would become a carpenter and fix the windows in the hut of a poor man. We understood that He sat upon the throne of the universe and angels and archangels bowed in adoration at His feet, but it never occurred to us that He would sit down and partake of a frugal meal among sun-burned. fishermen. We understood that He commanded all the mighty hosts of heaven, that angels flew on lightning wing, that at His look and word devils fled in consternation at His command, but we did not know that He would gather little children into His bosom and bless them with His caress and love.

Had Jesus not come to our earth, and lived with us here, had God not been manifest in the flesh, we never could have known the heart of the infinite Father. We are profoundly impressed, as never before, that there is closer kinship than we yet have dreamed, between God and His creature man, made in His image, redeemed by the incarnation and sufferings of His Son, adopted as His children, with the promise that we shall be satisfied when we awake in His likeness.

It seems to us that contemplation of these great facts in our holy religion

(62)

ought to lead to a universal rebellion against sin—a great heartcry for redemption from all of its effects, for restoration to purity of heart and holiness of life. The greatest need of our time is that we get away from mere theological theories and human philosophies about Christ and that we get back to Christ Himself. Not that Christ of men's notions, manufactured by this, that, and the other school of theology, but the Christ God gave to men; the Christ of the gospels, the Christ of Bethlehem, Nazareth, Galilee, Bethany, Jerusalem, Gethsemane, Calvary, Mt. Olivet; the Christ who lived and labored, hungered and suffered, loved and forgave, who died in tears and blood and agony on the cross for a sinful race.

The great Frederick W. Robertson, in his sermon on the sinlessness of Christ, makes this impressive statement: "There may be such an exclusive dwelling upon the divinity of Jesus as absolutely to destroy His real humanity; there may be such a morbid sensitiveness when we speak of Him, as taking our nature, as will destroy the fact of His sufferings—yes, and destroy the reality of His atonement also. There is a way of speaking of the sinlessness of Jesus that would absolutely make that scene on Calvary a mere pageant, in which He was acting a part in a drama, during which He was not really suffering, and did not really crush the propensities of His human nature."

Further on in the same sermon, he says: "Trust in divine humanity elevates the soul. It is done by hope. You must have observed the hopefulness of the character of Jesus—His hopefulness for human nature. If ever there were one who might have despaired, it was He. Full of love Himself, He was met with every sort of unkindness, every kind of derision. There was treachery in one of His disciples, dissension amongst them all. He was engaged in the hardest work that man ever tried. He was met by the hatred of the whole world, by torture and the cross; and yet never did the hope of Human Nature forsake the Redeemer's soul. He would not break the bruised reed, nor quench the smoking flax. There was a spark mingling even in the lowest Humanity, which He would fain have fanned into a blaze. The lowest publican Jesus could call to Him, and touch his heart; the lowest profligate that was ever trodden under foot by the world, was one for whom He could hope still. If he met with penitents, He would welcome them; if they were not penitents, but yet felt the pangs of detected guilt, still with hopefulness He pointed to forgiven Humanity; this was His word, even to the woman brought to Him by her accusers,—"Go, and sin no more;" in His last moments on the cross, to one who was dying by His side, He promised a place in Paradise: and the last words that broke from the Redeemer's lips, what were they but hope for our Humanity, while the curses were ringing in His ears?—"Father, forgive them, for they know not what they do."

We can no more permit the theologian and philosophers to rob us of the humanity of Jesus, than we can permit the destructive critic and skeptic to rob us of the deity of Jesus. We must keep in our thought, worship in our heart, and proclaim in our message to the people the Christ of the gospels, that human-divine being, who lived, walked and talked with the disciples; that human Christ who can be touched with the feelings of our infirmities; that divine Christ who is able to save to the uttermost, who is the same yesterday, today and forever.

Henry Van Dyke a few years ago delivered a lecture before the Divinity students of Yale University on the human life of God. This, with other lectures, he has bound up into a book entitled "The Gospel for an Age of Doubt." In the preface of this book, he says: "To seek Christ as the true Son of God, and the brother of all men, is to be sure that the soul is free, and that God is good, and that the end of life is noble service." In this lecture, to which we have referred, on the human life of God, Van Dyke says: "This complete incarnation, this thorough trial under human conditions, this perfect discipline of obedience through suffering was a humiliation. But it was in no sense a degradation. On the contrary, it was a crowning of Christ with glory and honor in order that He might taste death for every man. 'For it became Him, for whom are all things, and by whom are all things, in bringing many sons to glory, to make the Captain of their salvation perfect through suffering.' If the Epistle to the Hebrews teaches anything, it certainly teaches this. The humanity of Jesus was not the veiling but the unveiling of the divine glory. The limitations, temptations, and sufferings of manhood were the conditions under which alone Christ could accomplish the greatest work of the Deity—the redemption of a sinful race. The seat of the divine revelation and the center of the divine atonement was and is the human life of God."

The further we pursue our line of thought, the closer we come to Jesus Christ, the more profoundly we are impressed with the text—"Great is the mystery of godliness." This beautiful Babe of Bethlehem, this wondrous youth of twelve years, this patient carpenter of Nazareth, this meek and lowly man followed by ignorant fishermen, "Receiving sinners and eating with them," this matchless preacher of the truth, this majestic Master of devils, disease and death; this man in bloody sweat in Gethsemane, this victim of human hate and mob violence falling beneath His burden on Calvary's hillside, this white-faced, sinless Jesus hanging on the cross—Do you know who He is! He is God manifest in the flesh.

Do you ask what all of this means! It means that the good Shepherd of heaven has come to earth seeking His lost sheep. It means the redemption of sinners; it means that fallen men are to be born again and become in Christ new creatures. It means that the depraved and sinful are to become sanctified, that strangers to the commonwealth of Israel are to become the sons of God. It means that the demon-possessed are to sit clothed and in their right minds at the Master's feet. It means that this man of Galilee, this Jesus of Nazareth is God manifest in the flesh to save a lost race; that sinful men are to partake of the divine nature,

(69)

that the demon-possessed on their way to hell are to become pure and holy beings, are to walk in righteousness through the earth and to ascend in triumph to heaven. Wondrous Christ, mighty to save!

Jesus Christ belonged to no special race of men. He was the Son of man, the own full brother of every man of every race. His kinship with men helps us to love and hope for all men. He belonged to no special age. He belonged to all ages, to all time, to all eternity. He was with the Father before the world was. Abraham saw His day and was glad. Moses promises His coming. Micah tells us that He was to be born in Bethlehem. David sings of Him in a hundred Psalms, Isaiah describes His humble person, His patient suffering, His cruel death, and His final triumph.

The eternal God, in the person of His Son, got off the throne of the universe, came down into a wicked world, was born in a stable, lay in a manger, grew up in poverty, lived amid hardships, labored with His hands and suffered for the necessaries of His life. After the day of toil He had not where to lay His head. He conquered Satan. He overcame the prejudices of men. The wife of Pilate sent Him a message saying, "Have nothing to do with this just man." Pilate said, "I find in Him no fault at all." Judas Iscariot confessed, "I have betrayed innocent blood." The captain of the band who crucified Him on the cross said, "Certainly this was a righteous man."

The civilized world today acknowledges Him the Son of God. The heathen world begs to hear His gospel. The multitudes of earth ask to be baptized in His name and millions of redeemed souls are waiting with hope and prayer for His coming. We believe in Him, we worship Him, we pledge and con-

(71)

secrate our all to Him. We cry to the lost race—"Behold the Lamb of God, which taketh away the sin of the world." Our hearts respond to the poet who wrote,

"All hail the power of Jesus' name,
　Let angels prostrate fall;
Bring forth the royal diadem,
　And crown Him Lord of all.

"Let every kindred, every tribe
　On this terrestrial ball,
To Him all majesty ascribe,
　And crown Him Lord of all.

"Oh, that with yonder sacred throng,
　We at His feet may fall,
We'll join the everlasting song,
　And crown Him Lord of all."

www.ingramcontent.com/pod-product-compliance
Lightning Source LLC
Chambersburg PA
CBHW020515030426
42337CB00011B/406